The World
IN THE TIME OF
Tutankhamun

Belitha Press

Fiona Macdonald

First published in the UK in 1997 by

 Belitha Press Limited, London House, Great Eastern
Wharf, Parkgate Road, London SW11 4NQ

Copyright in this format © Belitha Press 1997
Text by Fiona Macdonald and Sarah McNeill
Map by Robin Carter, Wildlife Art Agency

ISBN 1 85561 558 4

British Library Cataloguing in Publication Data
for this book is available from the British Library.

Editor: Claire Edwards
Art Director: Helen James
Series Design: Roger Miller
Design: Juanita Grout, Rosamund Saunders and Jamie Asher
Picture Researcher: Diana Morris
Consultant: Sallie Purkis

Printed in Hong Kong

Picture acknowledgments:
Bridgeman Art Library: 1cl; 6-7t, 12 British Museum; 13b Sally Greene;
14r National Museum of India, New Delhi; 15t; 15c National Archaeological
Museum, Athens; 20l Louvre, Paris; 23r Museum of Mankind, London;
24 Giraudon; 25t Sally Greene; 25b Sally Greene; 27b National Archaeological
Museum, Athens; 35c British Museum; 35b National Museum of Australia,
Canberra; 36t Louvre, Paris; 36b Giraudon; 42r Giraudon/Louvre; 43b National
Museum of India, New Delhi; 44b National Archaeological Museum, Athens.
C.M.Dixon: 1c, 5c, 13t, 17b, 19t, 21t, 21c, 25b, 26b, 28l, 31b, 32t, 32c, 33bl,
37, 38t, 41t, 41b, 45b.
Werner Forman Archive: 5tl Egyptian Museum, Cairo; 17t Anthropology
Museum, Veracruz; 22b Provincial Museum, Victoria, B.C.; 33br, 39b British
Museum, London; 43t British Library, London.
Robert Harding Picture Library: front cover, 1cr, 2; 4, 5tr F.L. Kennett;
5b, 6b, 18, 20r; 25c V Southwell; 29t Christopher Rennie; 37t F.L. Kennett;
39t Gary Hansen; 40 F.L. Kennett; 42l.
Michael Holford: 7b; 14l Musée Cernuschi, Paris; 19b British museum;
27t, 30; 31c British Museum, London; 34.
N.J. Saunders: 45t.
South American Pictures: 16, 23t Tony Morrison.

CONTENTS

ABOUT THIS BOOK

This book tells the story of Tutankhamun, and also looks at what was happening all around the world in his time. To help you find your way through the book, each chapter has been divided into seven sections. Each section describes a different part of the world, and is headed by a colour bar. As you look through a chapter, the colour bars tell you which areas you can read about in the text below. There is a time line, to give you an outline of world events in Tutankhamun's time, and also a map, which shows some of the most important places mentioned in this book.

On page 46 there is a list of some of the peoples you will come across in this book. Some of the more unfamiliar words are also listed in the glossary.

THE STORY OF TUTANKHAMUN

Tutankhamun lived in Egypt almost 3,500 years ago. He was born around 1362 BC and became pharaoh when he was about nine years old. This book will tell you about life in Tutankhamun's Egypt, and what was happening elsewhere in the world in Tutankhamun's time. Because so many important things happened before and after Tutankhamun's short reign, this book also looks at a longer time span, from around 2000 to 1000 BC.

▼ The mask that covered the face of Tutankhamun's mummy. It is made of pure gold inlaid with semi-precious stones.

AN AMAZING DISCOVERY

Tutankhamun was very young when he became pharaoh, and his reign was short. He did not lead armies into battle, or make wise new laws. But today his name and his face are known all over the world. This is because his tomb survived untouched for thousands of years. When archaeologists finally opened it in 1922, they found it full of treasures like the gold portrait mask on the left. These grave goods tell us how rich the Egyptian pharaohs were, and show the amazing skills of the craftsmen and women who worked for them.

Tutankhamun is also remembered because his government paid for new temples and statues in many parts of the land, and rebuilt the old capital city of Thebes. His workers created some of Egypt's finest monuments, which we can still admire today.

◄ This carved stone panel shows Pharaoh Akhenaten (left), his wife Queen Nefertiti (right), and three of their daughters being blessed by the rays of Aten, the god of the sun.

▼ Two daggers, with their golden scabbards (cases), buried with Tutankhamun in his tomb.

A FAMILY OF KINGS

Tutankhamun's father was the pharaoh Amenophis III, one of the richest and most successful rulers in the whole of Egypt's history. His mother was Queen Tiye, a strong-minded and intelligent black princess from the rich kingdom of Nubia, south of Egypt. Tutankhamun was the youngest of their three sons and (probably) seven daughters. Because he had two older brothers he did not expect to rule.

◄ Young Tutankhamun probably looked like this carved wood and plaster portrait head, found in his tomb.

EARLY LIFE

In 1365 BC, when Tutankhamun was about three, he was sent to live in his oldest brother's palace. His brother's name was Akhenaten. Tutankhamun was brought up with Akhenaten's children.

Like other royal boys, Tutankhamun went to school. He had lessons every morning from palace scribes. They taught him to read the Egyptian picture-writing called hieroglyphs. He also learned how to write on papyrus (paper made from reeds), using a pen made from a goose feather and ink made from soot mixed with glue. In the afternoons, he practised swimming and wrestling, and was taught to hunt wild animals and fight in war.

◄ Earrings from Tutankhamun's tomb, made of gold and the semi-precious stones carnelian (orange-red), lapis lazuli (deep blue) and turquoise (greenish-blue). He would have worn these on special occasions.

A NEW RELIGION

When their father died, Tutankhamun's brother, Akhenaten, became pharaoh. Akhenaten was very different from his warlike father. His main interest was religion. He banned the old, magical temple ceremonies and dismissed the priests of Egypt's ancient gods. In their place, Akhenaten introduced new rituals for worshipping the god Aten – the life-giving sun. He even moved away from the old royal city of Thebes and built a whole new city, named Akhetaten, on the opposite bank of the River Nile.

CITY LIFE

Young Tutankhamun probably enjoyed life in Akhenaten's new city, with its palaces and gardens, feasts and festivals. Carvings in his tomb show that he honoured Aten, as well as the older, traditional gods, for the rest of his life.

Akhenaten's religious beliefs made the old priests and palace officials very angry. Akhenaten's wife left him, and many Egyptian people threatened to rebel. Tutankhamun's middle brother, Smenkhkare, helped Akhenaten govern the country, but Akhenaten and Smenkhkare both died early in 1352 BC. Now it was the turn of Tutankhamun to rule.

▲ This panel from a painted casket shows Tutankhamun hunting in the desert. He is armed with a bow and arrows, and is riding in a chariot pulled by four horses. Chariots like this were a new invention in Tutankhamun's time.

► Tutankhamun's royal throne. At the back you can see a jewelled panel showing Tutankhamun sitting down while his wife spreads perfume on his chest.

CROWNED AS A GOD

Tutankhamun was crowned in a splendid ceremony. Priests wore animal-headed masks to represent the gods. They led him through a dark, mysterious temple until he reached the holy throne (see left) where crowns were placed on his head. Once he had been crowned, Tutankhamun became both a god and the chief priest of Egypt.

A YOUNG PHARAOH

Tutankhamun was too young to rule the country. His vizier, Horhamreb, took charge, together with palace scribes and old, wise priests. Now Akhenaten was dead, they were powerful again. They removed Akenhaten's name from the temples he had built, and pulled down his new city. Tutankhamun went back to Thebes, where he lived in a fine new palace. There, he began to learn about laws and government, and how he should rule. Sadly, we will never know what sort of a pharaoh he would have been, because he died suddenly, aged about 19, in 1343 BC.

TUTANKHAMUN'S TOMB

Tutankhamun was buried in a tomb hidden deep in the hillside of the Valley of the Kings, Upper Egypt. His body was made into a mummy, then cased in a coffin coated with gold. His burial chamber was filled with everything that a dead pharaoh's spirit might need, from food and drink to books and board games. The tomb walls were covered with magical pictures (such as the hunting scene above) showing Tutankhamun's new life in the world of the dead. Much of our knowledge about ancient Egyptians and pharaohs comes from tomb paintings and goods like these.

◄ Many Egyptian gods were shown with animal heads and human bodies. This painting on papyrus shows a scene in the kingdom of the dead. The dog-headed Anubis is weighing a dead person's heart against a feather, to see how truthful they have been. The bird-headed god, Thoth, is writing down the result.

THE WORLD 2000–1000

ABOUT THE MAPS

The maps on this page will help you to find your way around. The big map shows some of the places and peoples mentioned in the text including:

• **COUNTRIES** that are different from modern ones, such as Canaan.

• *Past peoples*, such as the Hittites.

• **Towns and cities**. To find the position of a town or city look for the name in the list below then find the number on the map.

1	San Lorenzo	10	Ur
2	Chavin de Huantar	11	Akhetaten
3	La Venta	12	Karnak
4	Troy	13	Thebes
5	Mycenae	14	Deir el Medina
6	Knossos	15	Harappa
7	Çatal Hüyük	16	Mohenjo-Daro
8	Jericho	17	Lothal
9	Babylon	18	Anyang

The little map shows the world divided into seven regions. The people who lived there were linked by customs, beliefs, traditions, or simply by their environment, although there were many differences within each region. Each region is shown in a different colour. The same colours are used in the headings throughout the book to help you match the text with the region.

ARCTIC
OCEAN

BC

EUROPE
Celts

5

4 Hittites
Mycenaeans 7 Sumerians
Minoans 8 ASSYRIA
Phoenicians 9
6 CANAAN 10 MESOPOTAMIA
Jews

EGYPT

Hyksos 11

12

14 13

VALLEY OF
THE KINGS

NUBIA

SAHARA

A F R I C A

Bantu

CONGO

Khoisan

A S I A

Mongols

18

HUANG HE
SHANG CHINA

Indo-
Europeans 15
16
INDUS VALLEY
Aryans
17

PACIFIC
OCEAN

I N D I A N
O C E A N

Pacific peoples

Aboriginals

AUSTRALASIA

BLUE MOUNTAINS

I C A

KEY TO MAP

⬛	Africa
⬛	Americas
⬛	Australasia
⬛	East Asia
⬛	Europe
⬛	Middle East
⬛	South Asia

TIME LINE

| | 2000 BC | 1800 BC | 1600 BC |

AFRICA

2000–1000 Khoisan hunter-gatherers are the only inhabitants of South Africa.

1800 Shaduf used to irrigate fields in Egypt.

1800 Stoneworking industry develops in Ethiopia.

c.1700 Horse-drawn chariot introduced into Egypt.

1567–1090 New Kingdom era in Egypt.

MIDDLE EAST

2000 Sumerian power collapses, but soon begins to revive.

2000 Bronze in widespread use throughout the Middle East.

2000 Babylonians are using calendar based on 60-minute hour and 24-hour day.

1900 Ironworking techniques developed by Hittites in Turkey.

1800 King Shamsi-Addad founds Assyrian empire in Mesopotamia.

1800 First horse-drawn war chariots used in Middle East.

1792–1750 King Hammurabi rules Babylon.

1750–1200 Hittite empire is at height of its power in Turkey and nearby lands.

SOUTH ASIA

2000 In Thailand villagers hunt wild pigs and gather wild rice, and make fine pottery, bronze axes and jewellery.

1900 The last mud-brick temples built at Mohenjo-Daro in Indus Valley.

1700 New farming villages, growing wheat and rice, built in foothills of Himalayas.

1600 Mysterious Indus Valley picture-writing stops being used.

EAST ASIA

1900 First cities built in China.   **1766–1027** Shang Dynasty rules China.

2205–1766 Hsia Dynasty rules China.

c.2000 First silk-making in China.

1950 First zoo (called the 'Park of Intelligence') built in China.

1550 Bronze ploughs invented in Vietnam.

EUROPE

2000 First sails used on sea-going boats in the Mediterranean.

2000 Skilled bronzeworkers in many parts of Europe.

2000 First known skis in Scandinavia.

2000–1450 Minoan civilization in Crete is rich and powerful.

1650 Mycenean civilization grows strong in Greece.

1550 Last stages of rebuilding Stonehenge in England.

AMERICAS

2000 Guinea pigs first domesticated in South America.

1800 First South American villages built in Peru.

1800 Long distance trade networks established in north-east America.

AUSTRALASIA

2000 Aboriginal peoples move to settle in eastern Australia.

2000 Settlers from Indonesia reach Melanesia (western Pacific islands).

2000 Aboriginals in eastern Australia discover ways of processing poisonous fruit to use as food.

2000–1500 Dingoes (dogs) introduced into Australia, from South-east Asia or possibly India.

1500BC   **1200BC**   **1000BC**

1489–1469 Queen Hatshepsut rules Egypt.

1500 Village of Deir el Medina built in Egypt for workers building royal tombs.

1352 Tutankhamun becomes pharaoh.

1158 World's first recorded strike by builders working for pharaohs in Egypt.

1300 Earliest cereal-farming villages built in Kenya and Tanzania.

1290–1224 Pharaoh Ramesses II builds massive temple at Abu Simbel.

1200 Moses leads Jews from slavery in Egypt to new homeland in Israel.

1020 Jewish kingdom of Israel founded.

1100 Iron replaces bronze as the most important metal for weapons and tools.

1100 Phoenicians invent alphabet of letters on which modern European script is still based.

1500 Aryans invade northern India; they introduce bronze weapons and war chariots into India.

1000 Ironworking introduced to India.

1500 Horses, camels and donkeys introduced into northern India.

1400–1000 First bronze tools and simple drums made in Malaya, Indonesia, and also in Vietnam.

1500 Indus Valley civilization collapses.

1450 Hindu worship of god Brahman slowly spreads through India.

1500 Chinese use pictograph script (picture-writing).

1200 Bells cast from bronze made in China.

1500 Rice first grown using paddy-field (flooded field) system in Korea.

1200 Soya bean cultivation becomes widespread in China.

1100 Mouth organ invented in China.

1450 Mycenaeans invade Minoan Crete.

1250 Traditional date of Trojan War.

1250 Lion Gate built at Mycenae, Greece.

1200 End of Mycenaean civilization in Greece.

1000 Ironworking becomes widespread in Greece and Central Europe.

1400 Sunflowers first cultivated in North America.

1500 First Maya people settle in clearings in the rainforests of Guatemala.

1200 Chavin civilization develops in Peru.

1000 New Adena civilization in Ohio valley in North America.

1500 Earliest metalwork in South America.

1200 Beginnings of Olmec civilization in Mexico.

1300 Settlers from New Guinea migrate to Fiji.

1000 Long distance trade routes develop in Australia.

1500 Aboriginal hunters invent new kinds of traps for fish and eels.

1100 Settlers from Fiji reach Tonga and Samoa.

Many of the dates shown in this Time Line are approximate.

AROUND THE WORLD

The world was a very restless place in Tutankhamun's time. In some parts, such as Egypt and China, there were civilizations that had existed in one place for thousands of years. Often these had grown up along river valleys, where there was plenty of fertile land. People settled there, and built towns that grew into big cities with powerful rulers. But in many other regions – southern Africa, Asia, Europe and the Pacific – groups of migrating peoples were on the move, in search of a new home.

Sometimes small tribes fought richer neighbours just for a share of good land. But most migrations were on a very large scale. For example, the Indo-European peoples left their home in southern Russia to settle in India, Greece, Central Europe and Iran. Often migrants attacked and conquered earlier civilizations, setting up new nations and introducing their own language, technology and beliefs.

◄ This stone pillar was used to mark the borders of a rich man's land. It shows King Nebuchadnezzar I, who ruled Babylon around 1140 BC, together with gods and monsters.

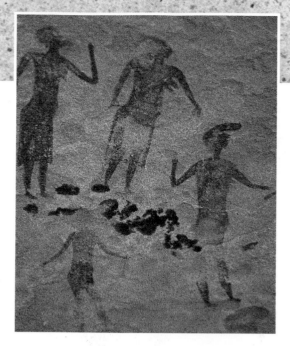

▲ A cave painting from Algeria. It shows men and women in dry countryside on the borders of the Sahara Desert. It was probably painted between 5000 and 1000 BC.

TOWNS AND EMPIRES

MIDDLE EAST

The first towns in the world were built in the Middle East, at Çatal Hüyük (in Turkey) and Jericho (in Jordan), between around 8000 and 6500 BC. They were both important centres for religion, crafts and trade. Çatal Hüyük was abandoned about 5000 BC, but Jericho was still rich and busy in Tutankhamun's day. By then it had been rebuilt and enlarged many times.

After around 2000 BC, Babylon, in Mesopotamia (part of present-day Iraq) became the most important town in the Middle East. It was the capital city of a great empire founded by King Hammurabi (see page 20), who ruled from 1792 to 1750 BC.

WEALTH AND POWER

AFRICA

Tutankhamun lived during an era called the New Kingdom, which lasted from 1567 to 1090 BC. It began when Egyptian armies drove invaders, called the Hyksos, out of their land. After that, Egyptian pharaohs, including Tutankhamun's father, set out to rebuild their kingdom's wealth and power. They conquered an empire that stretched from present-day Sudan to the borders of Turkey. They built huge monuments to thank the gods for their success, and as memorials to their own power. You can see a pharaoh attacking his enemies in the stone carving (right).

NATIONS ON THE MOVE

In some parts of Africa, whole nations were on the move. A change in the climate made the Sahara region drier, so the peoples living there moved south in search of better grazing for their flocks of sheep and herds of horses and cattle. Groups of Bantu people from the forests of West Africa also left their homes to look for new land. They travelled south through the Congo valley, and eastwards towards the coast.

► In this stone carving Pharaoh Ramesses III is killing an enemy with a war club. Underneath craftsworkers carved the names of cities he conquered.

THE SHANG EMPIRE

EAST ASIA

In northern China, a powerful empire grew up in the fertile Huang He (Yellow River) valley, ruled by emperors from the Shang Dynasty. Skilled craftworkers, priests and scribes lived in the empire's rich cities. Below, there is an example of fine Shang craftwork.

In the countryside peasants farmed wheat and millet. Rice was grown in the empire's warmest, rainiest lands. Fierce warriors rode about in horse-drawn chariots, keeping control of conquered peoples. They also helped the emperors defend the empire from invaders, such as the Mongol tribes from the north.

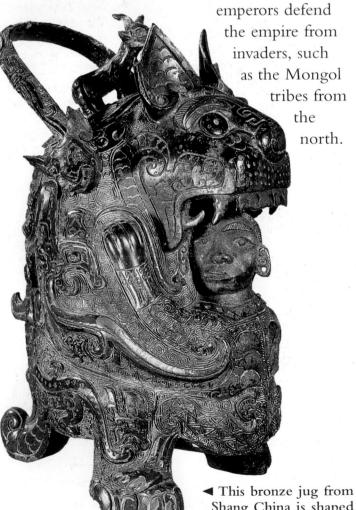

◀ This bronze jug from Shang China is shaped like a tiger. It was used to hold wine, which was poured out as an offering to dead ancestors. This was an important part of religious worship.

THE INDUS VALLEY

SOUTH ASIA

From around 2500 BC, the Indus Valley (in present-day northern India and Pakistan) was home to a great civilization. The people who lived there were traders and lived in towns. More than a hundred sites have been discovered so far, scattered over a vast area of about a million square kilometres. The biggest cities, such as Mohenjo-Daro, Harappa and Lothal, had streets that were carefully laid out on a grid plan, and complicated drainage systems. There were also huge grain stores, palaces and ceremonial baths. Town dwellers had money to spend on art and entertainment, as the little statue of a richly-jewelled dancing girl (see right) shows.

The Indus Valley civilization collapsed around 1500 BC. No one knows why. It may have been destroyed by invading tribes. Or it may have been destroyed by a change in the climate, by earthquakes, or by floods.

▶ A copper statue of a dancing girl. It is about 14 centimetres high, and was made by craftworkers from the city of Harappa in the Indus Valley, around 2000 BC.

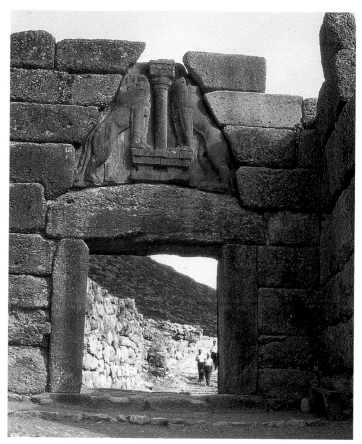

▲ The Lion Gate at the entrance to the king's palace at Mycenae, southern Greece. The gateway and the lions above it are made from huge blocks of stone.

GREEK WARRIOR KINGS

On the Greek mainland, proud warrior kings ruled rival city-states. A city-state was a city or town, together with the surrounding farms and fields. Greek kings defended their land by building strong forts with massive gateways, like the one you can see on the left. They led their armies to attack Minoan Crete in 1450 BC, and waged a famous war against the city of Troy (in present-day Turkey) around 1250 BC.

◄ Noblewomen in Minoan Crete wore elegant clothes. This fresco (wall-painting) is from a royal palace. It shows a young woman wearing a fitted top and a long full skirt. Her dark curly hair is loose, and she has large hoop-shaped earrings.

MINOAN STYLE

EUROPE

In southern Europe, from around 2000 BC, Minoan people lived in great comfort and style on the island of Crete. You can see a glamorous Minoan noblewoman in the picture on the right. The Minoans ruled an empire that included many Mediterranean islands, as well as city-states on the shores of southern and central Greece. They traded with the Egyptians and Middle Eastern peoples, and sometimes fought against them, too. Minoan power was weakened after a volcano called Thera erupted on an island near Crete around 1450 BC. Dust from the volcano blotted out the sun, damaged the land and caused a shortage of food.

FARMERS AND HUNTERS

In northern Europe there were no cities. Instead farmers and hunters lived in villages and farms. Because they left no written records, we do not know much about their society. But grave goods show us that there were a few very rich people, probably warrior chiefs. There were lots of rich merchants too, who traded in amber and gold.

Around 1200 BC, early Celtic settlers arrived from eastern Europe, bringing with them a new civilization. The Celts built forts on the tops of hills, and traded with southern Europe for wine.

RIVER VALLEYS: SETTLED VILLAGES

AMERICAS

In Tutankhamun's time, there were many different civilizations in North and South America. These included the Inuit seal hunters of the icy Arctic north and the peoples of the steamy Amazon rainforest, who survived by gathering insects and wild plants. Many of these hunters lived nomadic lives, always moving on to new land in search of food. But by Tutankhamun's time, some Native American peoples had settled in sheltered, well-watered river valleys, where they built villages, cleared fields, and planted crops.

In the wide valleys of the Mississippi and Ohio rivers, people lived by farming sunflowers, gourds and pumpkins, and by long-distance trade. Around 1100 BC they began to build massive earthworks, which they used as religious meeting places and for defence.

A SPLENDID MEXICAN CITY

In Mexico, the Olmec civilization became powerful around 1200 BC. Its capital city and religious centre was at San Lorenzo. The Olmecs controlled rich farmlands. Unlike many other parts of Mexico, crops grew very well there and harvests were good, thanks to flood water from rivers and seasonal rains. Because of this the Olmec people rarely went short of food. Their population increased, and the Olmec nation grew strong and wealthy.

The Olmec rulers of San Lorenzo paid for many enormous monuments to be built, such as earth-mound temples, ceremonial lakes and stone thrones. Craftworkers also carved eight colossal heads, each one of a different king. Archaeologists have found the remains of over 200 houses in the centre of San Lorenzo. This suggests that well over 1,000 people lived there, making San Lorenzo one of the biggest cities of the time.

▲ These well-armed warriors were carved on to stone at a ceremonial centre in Peru known as Chavin de Huantar.

MOUNTAIN HOMES

From around 2000 BC, people began to build the first villages in South America, in the Andes region. By around 1200 BC, these villages had stone temples, open air meeting spaces, and channels bringing water from mountain streams. Most had markets where mountain produce such as potatoes, could be exchanged for fish and shells from the coast. Warriors guarded the villages and helped rulers to take control of more land.

▲ A massive head carved from stone by Olmec craftworkers at San Lorenzo. It is more than 2 metres high and weighs 20 tonnes. It shows an Olmec king wearing a helmet.

EXPLORING NEW LAND

AUSTRALASIA

The Aboriginal people first settled in Australia around 40,000 BC. At first they lived along the coast, but as the sea level rose and flooded their homes, they moved inland. They travelled from camp to camp as they hunted and explored. By Tutankhamun's time they had made a network of long-distance routes between camp sites, holy places and hunting grounds. Aboriginal sailors also traded with India and South Asian lands.

UNINHABITED ISLANDS

At first no one lived on the islands of the Pacific Ocean. But around 2000 BC, groups of people left their homelands in South-East Asia, Indonesia and Papua New Guinea, and set off towards the unknown, in search of more food and new land. They made long, dangerous ocean journeys, sometimes over 2,500 kilometres, in fragile wooden canoes. To help them navigate, they watched wind and wave patterns, the flight of seabirds and the movement of clouds and the stars. Soon after Tutankhamun's time they had reached Fiji, Tonga and Samoa, and had set up thriving communities there. The Pacific settlers brought many ideas and customs from their old homelands, including belief in spirits like the ones pictured below.

▼ Ancient spirit faces painted on the wall of a modern house in Papua New Guinea. Beliefs in spirits like these have survived since Tutankhamun's time.

FAMOUS RULERS AND LEADERS

Today, in democratic countries, if people do not like the way their rulers behave, they can vote to remove them from power. But in Tutankhamun's time, whether rulers were good or bad, they usually stayed in power for life. Most rulers claimed that the gods had given them the right to run the country. Some believed that they were descended from the gods, or were gods themselves.

In lands such as Egypt and the Middle East, scribes proudly recorded the deeds of their rulers. In other parts of the world, myths and legends tell us the names of early kings. But in many regions no written records were kept. We do not know the names of the rulers who lived there. But by looking carefully at archaeological remains and ancient traditions we can discover some of the things they did.

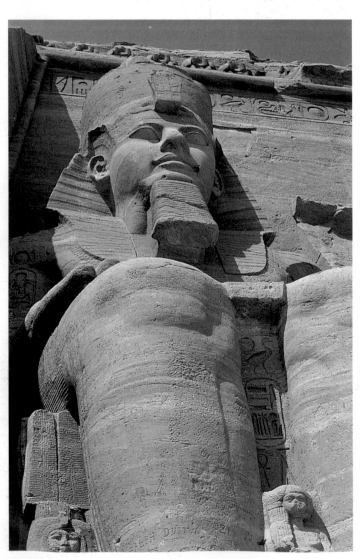

◄ This huge statue of Ramesses II is carved out of solid rock. It stands outside his most famous temple at Abu Simbel in southern Egypt. The temple was specially built so that twice a year the sun's rays shone through the doorway, showing statues of the gods carved on the inner walls.

RULERS OF THE GODS

The Egyptians were taught that their pharaohs were gods in human form. Pharaohs were worshipped, respected and feared. As chief priests, war leaders and guardians of law and order, they had many duties. They planned conquests, made peace treaties and gave orders to thousands of government officials. Many of Egypt's greatest rulers lived in the New Kingdom period, for example Queen Hatshepsut (1498–1483 BC), who ruled on behalf of her stepson, Pharaoh Tuthmosis III. Even when he was grown up, she refused to hand over power. Under her rule, Egypt began to trade with and explore distant lands.

◄ Queen Hatshepsut had a huge temple built as a memorial to herself on the the banks of the River Nile. This statue of the queen is from the temple.

RAMESSES THE GREAT

Ramesses II lived from 1290 to 1224 BC and was one of Egypt's greatest pharaohs. He ruled for nearly 67 years, had 90 children, and left more monuments than any other Egyptian king. He fought long wars against the Hittites, and scenes from his battles were cut in stone in many of Ramesses' temples. Ramesses finally made peace with the Hittites in 1286 BC, and married a Hittite princess. To strengthen friendship between nations, many pharaohs married hundreds of official wives.

► A panel made to decorate a musical instrument called a lyre. The King of Sumer, at the top, receives enemy prisoners. Sumer is shown at the height of its power. By Tutankhamun's time, Sumerian power had collapsed, and Egypt and Babylon were the strongest powers in the Middle East.

WAR LEADERS

Rival tribes constantly fought over the lands of the Middle East, which meant that the earliest rulers were war leaders. Victory in war brought vast riches, and some of these treasures were buried with kings when they died. Some of the most splendid royal tombs were built at Ur, capital of the Sumerian Empire. The empire was destroyed by invaders some time around 2000 BC.

WARRIOR AND LAW-MAKER

MIDDLE EAST

King Hammurabi (1792–1750 BC) was a successful warrior. He conquered a vast empire, which he ruled from the city of Babylon. But he became even more famous as a law-maker. He collected together all the laws from different parts of his empire, and arranged them in one single code. This code covered everything from robbery and murder to fair trade, paying doctors, getting married, hiring workers and buying slaves. Hammurabi ordered his laws to be carved on a tall stone pillar, which you can see below.

► Here you can see a stone portrait of a ruler-priest, from the city of Mohenjo-Daro. He is wearing a jewelled headband and armband, and an embroidered robe.

◄ This stele (stone pillar) shows the Babylonian sun-god Shamash dictating laws to King Hammurabi. The lower part of the pillar is carved with Hammurabi's laws. They ordered harsh punishments for anyone who disobeyed them.

RULER PRIESTS

SOUTH ASIA

The Indus Valley civilization was rich and well organized, with strongly built, carefully planned cities. This suggests that there were good leaders, but we do not know their names. The largest Indus Valley cities had homes for 40,000 people, with wide streets leading to huge religious buildings at the city centres. But no remains of palaces have been found. Historians think this means that the Indus Valley rulers were priests, rather than kings.

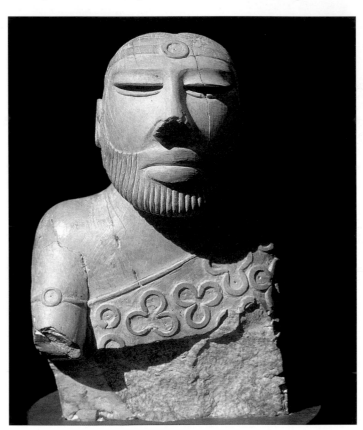

THE ARYANS

Around 1500 BC, the Aryans invaded northern India. We know about their society from a series of poems called the Vedas, some of the oldest surviving poems in the world. The Vedas describe a society led by kings and warrior heroes, organized into four separate groups called castes. Each caste had a different task to perform, as priests, warriors, merchants or farmers.

◄ This is the throne room in the royal palace at Knossos on the island of Crete. The palace was built for Minoan kings, but we do not know if King Minos existed in real life. He may be only a name in ancient stories and legends.

▼ A gold mask covering the face of a dead king, found in a tomb at Mycenae in Greece. At first, archaeologists thought it might belong to King Agamemnon, but in fact it was made for a king who died earlier.

HERO KINGS

EUROPE

We do not know the name of any northern European rulers who lived in Tutankhamun's time, but archaeologists have found their remains in huge stone tombs. We know more about rulers in southern Europe from Greek legends. The remains of palaces and tombs also survive in many parts of Greece.

According to Greek legend, King Minos was the ruler of Crete. His name is used to describe the civilization that survived there from around 2000–1450 BC. Four huge Minoan palaces have been found. The largest, at Knossos, had over 1,300 rooms, including the king's throne room, storerooms, bathrooms and lavatories. Many rooms were beautifully decorated with brightly-painted walls.

POWERFUL PRIESTESSES

Women often played an important part in decision-making in Mediterranean lands. As priestesses they gave advice to rulers, and even claimed to be able to see into the future. In Troy, the royal priestess Cassandra gave accurate warnings that her city would be destroyed in war.

THE TROJAN WAR

Ancient Greek poems describe a war fought around 1250 BC, between the Greeks and the Trojans, who lived in present-day Turkey. The poems say that King Agamemnon of Mycenae was leader of the Greeks. At Mycenae, there are the remains of a royal fortress, built on a hilltop and protected by huge gates (see page 15). King Agamemnon probably lived there. Similar fortress cities have been found elsewhere in Greece.

A LEGENDARY KING

EAST ASIA

According to ancient legends, the first Chinese ruler was Yu the Great, king of the Hsia Dynasty. But, because there are no written records, we cannot prove that he ever lived. We know more about the next ruling family, because Chinese scholars invented picture-writing during their reign. These kings belonged to the Shang Dynasty, and came to power around 1766 BC. The Shang kings ruled with the help of vast armies and fierce warlords. They encouraged crafts, farming, building and new technology, but many Chinese people thought them cruel.

▲ This imaginary portrait of Yu the Great was painted by a Chinese artist who lived thousands of years after King Yu's reign.

BURIALS AND SACRIFICES

In one of the Shang Dynasty's capital cities, called Anyang, archaeologists have found the remains of a magnificent royal palace. It stands on top of a huge burial pit containing 852 people, 35 dogs, 18 sheep, 15 horses, 10 oxen and 5 war chariots. They were all sacrificed before the palace was built, to bring good fortune to the Shang kings.

SKILFUL CHIEFS

AMERICAS

Rulers in North and South America had different duties, depending on how their people lived. Some were brave fighters, others were clever hunters, others were healers and priests, called shamans. Many Native American peoples were led by teams of chiefs. They were usually experienced warriors and wise men. Each member of the ruling team offered their own experience and skills to help the community survive. Some Native American leaders claimed to have magical powers that let them communicate with the spirit world.

► This mask has a human face and an eagle beak. The Native American Bella Coola people believed that four carpenters were told by their Creator to carve the very first humans. They flew to earth disguised as birds and animals. This is one of the carpenters.

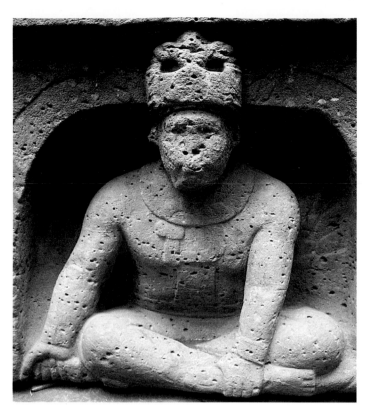

▲ A royal throne from the Olmec city of La Venta, Mexico. It is carved with the figure of a king wearing a large crown and a necklace.

KINGS AND CAPTIVES

Leaders of other American peoples, such as the Olmecs of Mexico, were army commanders and priests. They organized soldiers to defend their peoples' homes and farms, and to conquer new territory. They were also in charge of planting crops and sharing out food. They made laws to help villagers live peacefully with each other. Often, the palaces where they lived were places of worship as well as splendid homes. It was the duty of the leaders to kill captives taken in battle and to offer them to the gods.

From the evidence of massive statues, Olmec kings may have taken part in sacred ball games. In these games the movement of the ball was supposed to copy the movement of the sun as it travelled across the sky. Winners became heroes, but losers were killed as sacrifices.

RULERS FROM THE SEA

AUSTRALASIA

We do not know the names of any people who lived in Australia or the Pacific Islands in Tutankhamun's time. But in Australia, myths tell of a god-leader called the Djanggawul Brother. He arrived from the sea with his two sisters and taught the Aboriginal people to dig waterholes and find food. He also taught them new religious ceremonies. Real leaders probably behaved in this way, too.

Among the Pacific Islanders, the most powerful people may have been the leaders of groups of settlers who led their families and friends across the ocean in search of new land.

► A wooden statue of a sea god from islands in the Pacific Ocean. He is covered with tiny humans as a sign of his great strength and power. People made offerings to gods like these, asking for their protection in unknown lands.

HOW PEOPLE LIVED

All around the world civilizations had to produce enough food to feed their growing populations. Reliable supplies of food and water were especially important for craftworkers, merchants, government officials and other town dwellers. These people no longer grew their own food, but had to buy it instead.

Although towns were increasingly important, most people still lived in the countryside. Some were hunters and gatherers. Many more were farmers. All the world's major food crops, including wheat, maize, rice and yams, had been cultivated by around 1500 BC. Most farm animals, including cows, pigs, sheep, goats, horses and dogs, had been domesticated. But rulers and farmers were always looking for better ways to farm and extra crops to grow.

▼ In this Egyptian wall-painting, you can see a farmer and his wife hard at work. He is steering a plough pulled by two oxen. She is scattering seeds of corn. At the bottom of the picture there are date-palm trees, planted beside an irrigation ditch.

A RICH LAND

Tutankhamun lived in one of the richest countries on earth. Most of Egypt's land was desert, but every year the River Nile flooded its banks, spreading a layer of sticky black mud on either side. This fertile soil produced good crops of wheat, barley, fruit and vegetables. People called Egypt 'the gift of the Nile'. The Egyptians also sent teams of soldiers and miners to work gold and copper mines in nearby lands.

Pharaohs and top government officials lived in grand palaces, with dining halls, shower rooms, flower-filled gardens and ponds. Ordinary people lived in one-roomed houses of sun-dried mud brick, with stairs leading to a flat roof where they could sleep on hot nights.

Because Egypt was hot all year round, people wore few clothes. Children usually wore nothing at all, men wore loincloths or short skirts and women wore loose robes. Clothes were made of fine linen or of hemp. Men and women shaved their heads, possibly to get rid of lice. They wore thick wigs, which they perfumed on festival days.

HUNTERS AND GATHERERS

In Tutankhamun's time, the first farming villages were built in West Africa, Kenya and Tanzania. People built houses of earth, with roofs made of grass and leaves. In other parts of Africa, most people lived by gathering wild foods, by hunting in rainforests or by fishing. The far south of Africa was almost uninhabited, apart from a few bands of Khoisan hunters and gatherers.

▲ This cave-painting of a cow is from North Africa and was made between about 6000 and 1000 BC. Herdsmen grazed cattle on the edges of the Sahara Desert. They also gathered wild fruit and grains to eat.

◄ Rich Egyptian homes were full of lovely objects. Here craftsmen make gold and silver vases. First they hammer a vase into shape, then decorate it with engraved patterns, and finally they give it a polish.

BREAD, OIL AND WINE

In the marshy soils of Mesopotamia, farmers grew wheat, vegetables and fruit. They kept oxen to pull ploughs and caught fish and water-birds in irrigation ditches and canals. They built houses of reeds and sun-dried mud brick, dug from the river banks.

On higher ground, in Canaan and Assyria, farmers grew barley for bread, sesame for oil, and grape vines to make wine. On mountain slopes they tended forests of cedar trees. The sweet-smelling wood from these trees was used to decorate rich homes, palaces and temples in many Middle Eastern lands.

BUSTLING TOWNS

Busy, prosperous trading towns where scribes, merchants, doctors, lawyers and craftsworkers lived and worked could be found in many parts of the Middle East. Kings also built huge palaces, fine gardens and splendid temples.

Rich town people lived a leisurely life. In Mesopotamia, royal tombs have been found containing all sorts of objects, from board games to musical instruments. Women wore gold rings on their fingers and in their hair, and beads made of a red stone called carnelian. They also used make-up, which was kept in little shells.

BATHROOMS AND BRONZE

Indus Valley homes were built of mud bricks. They were large and well-planned, with five or six rooms arranged around a central courtyard. In towns they had piped water, and bathrooms and lavatories connected to a central drainage system – the most advanced in the world. Lothal, a city on the coast, was the main port. It had a brick-built harbour and big warehouses. Indus Valley merchants exchanged local products, such as timber, elephant ivory, spices and cotton cloth, for semi-precious stones, and tin, which they needed to make bronze.

◄ A large meeting-house built from reeds. This photo was taken in present-day Iraq, but reed houses were already being built in this style in Tutankhamun's time.

RICH LAND

Crops grew well in the Indus Valley. Farmers harvested wheat, fruit and vegetables from irrigated land, and hunted wild antelope and deer. They reared oxen and buffalo to pull ploughs and provide milk. They were the first people to grow cotton. Women picked its fluffy fibres, then spun and wove them to make cloth. Along the coast, cotton was also used to make strong fishing nets.

▲ These huge storage jars were found in a royal palace in Crete. They are about 2 metres high and were made to hold oil and grain.

FISHING AND POTTERY

In southern Europe, most people were farmers or fishermen. Farmers grew barley, grapes and olives. Fishermen caught mackerel, tuna, octopus and squid. There were also many craftworkers, who lived in towns. Cretan craftworkers made huge pottery jars, called pithoi, for storing oil, grain and wine. They also made brightly-decorated vases, gold and ivory jewellery and bronze swords. These were sold in Greece, Egypt and Middle Eastern lands. In Greece and Crete towns were built on hilltops, and surrounded by strong stone walls. Town houses were two or three storeys high.

► This wall-painting, or fresco, from Knossos in Crete, shows a young fisherman with his catch.

◄ Clay models like this ox-cart were made as toys and as religious offerings. They tell us what farm life was like in the Indus Valley.

FARMING LIFE

In northern Europe there were no towns. People lived in villages and small farms. Farmers had to cut down the dense forests before they could clear fields and plant crops of wheat and barley. Farmers kept cattle, sheep and goats for meat, milk, hides and wool. They built their houses from local materials such as stone or timber, with reed or straw-thatched roofs. Farming families also ate wild foods, such as birds' eggs, fish from rivers and the sea, and mushrooms, raspberries, hazelnuts and plums. In the forests they hunted deer and boar with spears.

FAMILIES

EAST ASIA

The Shang kings ruled a vast empire based in China's Huang He (Yellow River) valley. The soil was rich and fertile, although buildings and people were often swept away by earthquakes and floods. Most people lived in large villages, surrounded by deep ditches for defence. Parents, children, grandparents, cousins, uncles and aunts all lived together. Traditionally, the happiest homes had five generations all living under one roof.

▲ In regions where there was not much stone, Chinese builders made walls out of pounded earth supported by a wooden framework. This picture was painted around AD 100, but it shows how houses were built even before Tutankhamun's time.

RICH AND POOR

The nobles of China lived a luxurious life. They wore silk clothes and their houses were full of rich goods, such as bronze jugs and mirrors, and even jade scoops to clean their ears. Bronze was a new invention and was too special to use for farm tools, so peasants still worked using tools made of stone and wood. Peasants wore simple tunics and trousers made of hemp. In the north, where it was cold, they wore thick, padded jackets. Chinese farmers had to pay a tax to their landlord, or give him a share of their crops. They also had to work for the government for one month every year.

► Rich farmers built watchtowers to guard their land. This clay model was made in about 200 BC, but watchtowers like this were being built hundreds of years earlier.

◄ On the steep slopes of the Andes, farmers cut terraces like the ones in this picture to plant their crops of potatoes and maize.

▼ An Aboriginal eel-trap, made of woven rushes and willow twigs. Traps like these were hidden among the reeds at the edge of shallow rivers and lakes. This picture was sketched by a nineteenth-century traveller, but archaeologists believe this way of catching eels was invented in Tutankhamun's time.

THE NORTH

AMERICAS

The first inhabitants of America arrived in Alaska from Siberia around 30,000 BC. By Tutankhamun's time, they had settled throughout America. In the Arctic north, hunters killed caribou and polar bear with stone-tipped spears. In the hot, dry south-west, families built shelters out of twigs and gathered nuts, seeds and grubs. On the Great Plains, hunters tracked herds of buffalo. They lived in villages during the winter, and in the summer they lived in tepee camps. In the Mississippi valley, farmers caught fish and grew squash and sunflowers. They crushed the sunflower seeds to make oil.

EDIBLE DOGS AND GUINEA-PIGS

On the dry hillsides of Mexico, the main crop was maize. In the hot, wet valleys farmers grew avocados, beans, tomatoes and chillies, and reared turkeys and dogs to eat. Ordinary peoples' homes were made of earth with roofs thatched with leaves. Rulers lived in fine palaces made of stone.

In the Andes, farmers lived in houses made of rough-hewn stone. They dug irrigation channels and planted crops of potatoes and maize. They also reared guinea-pigs for food, llamas to carry heavy loads, and alpaca, for their warm wool.

MOTHS AND EELS

AUSTRALASIA

The Aboriginal people of Australia lived as nomads. They gathered wild seeds, berries and roots, trapped eels and fish, and hunted kangaroos with boomerangs. By 2000 BC they were moving into the highlands on the east coast, where they learned to survive on new foods. They roasted moths, and learned how to make the fruit of a poisonous palm safe to eat by slicing it and soaking it in water.

DISCOVERY AND INVENTION

The years from about 2000 to 1200 BC are often called the Bronze Age, because widespread use of bronze from about 2000 BC changed people's lives. Bronze is a metal – a mixture of 90 per cent copper and 10 per cent tin. Metalworkers in Asia, western Europe and the Middle East all discovered how to make it at about the same time.

Before bronze was invented, people used knives and weapons made of wood, or of copper or stone. But copper was very soft, and stone was heavy and difficult to shape. Bronze was much harder and sharper than copper, and could be hammered and moulded into intricate shapes. Metalworkers used it to make better, stronger swords, shields, daggers, helmets and spears.

▼ This wall-painting from an Egyptian tomb shows a boat on the River Nile. The boat moves with the help of the rowers and by wind trapped in the big square sail.

WATER ENGINEERS

AFRICA

Egyptian civilization was already 2,000 years old in Tutankhamun's time. For hundreds of years Egyptian farmers had dug canals and ditches to control the flow of water from the River Nile, and built huge tanks to store flood water for use in dry seasons. In about 1800 BC they invented a machine called a shaduf, which raised water from ditches and rivers to water their fields.

BUILDING TECHNOLOGY

The Egyptians were expert builders. The great pyramids, where earlier pharaohs were buried, are still wonders of the world. But the biggest building projects of Tutankhamun's time were new cities, temples, palaces and underground tombs. Builders had only simple tools such as chisels and mallets but they used them with great skill. They drew accurate plans on papyrus, and measured building sites with knotted ropes. They raised huge blocks of stone to the top of buildings by hauling them up ramps of pounded earth.

◄ A scroll of papyrus showing calculations made by an Egyptian mathematician around 1600 BC. On the left there are rules for measuring pyramids, angles and triangles. On the right, instructions for surveying land.

SUNDIALS AND MEDICINE

To measure time and record events, the Egyptians invented water-clocks, sundials and picture-writing called hieroglyphs. These were not all new in Tutankhamun's day, but they were always being improved. Mummy-making had also become a more complicated process. As well as preserving bodies, the Egyptians also studied them scientifically and recorded their findings in papyrus scrolls. These were written for doctors and gave details of diseases, treatments and medicines. Doctors learned a great deal about how the body is made, and also believed that the heart was the centre of the body.

◄ An obelisk (tall stone pillar) from the temple at Karnak, Egypt. It was built by Pharaoh Thutmose III, who ruled from 1504 to 1450 BC. It displays the pharaoh's name and his deeds in hieroglyphs.

◀ Babylonian copper farming equipment, including sickles, knives and axes, made around 1550 BC. Old-style tools like these were used before bronze and iron tools were invented.

▼ The Babylonians used their mathematical skills for measuring and surveying land. This clay tablet, written in cuneiform (wedge-shaped writing) was made around 1980 BC. It records the size of five fields.

ASTRONOMERS AND IRON

In Babylon, Hammurabi's laws (see page 20) said that doctors were expected to follow a strict medical code. The Babylonians were also skilled astronomers. By 2000 BC they had worked out ways of measuring time, using a 60-minute hour and a 24-hour day, which we still use today.

Some of the most important Middle Eastern inventions were designed for war. Around 1800 BC soldiers invented a wheeled battle-chariot, pulled by fast horses. By Tutankhamun's time, it had been copied by the Egyptians and other neighbouring countries.

In about 1900 BC, metalworkers in Syria and Turkey discovered how to make weapons and farm tools out of iron. This gave them a great advantage in building and farming, as well as in war. Iron was stronger, sharper, longer-lasting and more plentiful than bronze or copper. But for a while it was so rare and valuable – more precious than gold – that only a few people worked with it. Iron only became widely used throughout the Middle East by about 1100 BC.

A NEW ALPHABET

Around 1100 BC, the Phoenicians developed two important inventions. They discovered how to produce purple dye using sea-snails and a chemical called alum, dug from rocks. The dye was very valuable and selling it made them rich.

But their second invention was even more important. They invented an alphabet of letters. It soon replaced earlier ways of writing based on pictures (in Egypt) or patterns of little wedge shapes (in Mesopotamia). The Phoenician alphabet consisted of 22 letters. They were all consonants. Vowels were added later by Greek scholars. We still use the Phoenician alphabet today, in a modern form.

DAMS AND DRAINS

SOUTH ASIA

The people living in the Indus Valley, like the Egyptians and the Mesopotamians, depended on the River Indus for their survival and became skilled water engineers. They were among the first people to build dams to control the flow of water, and surrounded their fields with irrigation ditches. They also used careful measurements and engineering to plan and build their big cities. These had complicated underground networks of freshwater pipes and drains. They invented a system of writing, using picture-symbols scratched on tablets of damp clay. But a great mystery still surrounds this picture-writing. No one has yet been able to work out what it means.

► Chinese designs were copied by craftworkers in South Asia. In Thailand they created beautiful pottery like this vase using very simple methods. They did not have potters' wheels so every pot was carefully smoothed into shape and decorated by hand.

SILK AND BRONZE

EAST ASIA

In Tutankhamun's time, China was isolated from many other parts of the world. The Chinese did not know about inventions in Egypt and the Middle East. But they made their own discoveries, to meet their own needs.

According to Chinese legends, the king of Hsia (see page 22) taught people how to control floods, dig irrigation ditches, grow crops and make medicines. His wife showed people how to spin silk from the cocoons of insect grubs. Chinese people knew about all these things by around 2000 BC. Soon afterwards they invented wheeled chariots for war. They also invented the potters' wheel (also invented in Mesopotamia).

By around 1500 BC, Chinese metalworkers had discovered how to make beautiful vessels out of bronze. Scribes invented a system of picture-writing which is still used as the basis of Chinese script.

By 1000 BC, they had compiled a dictionary with 40,000 different characters. Chinese scholars also made mathematical discoveries, including an early form of 'times tables'.

► This Chinese axe head may have been carried by royal bodyguards, and was probably fixed to a wooden handle with leather straps. It was made by pouring melted bronze into a clay mould.

MASSIVE MONUMENTS

In northern Europe huge monuments, such as Stonehenge, were enlarged or rebuilt in Tutankhamun's time. Workers had no cranes or pulleys to lift the massive blocks of stone. Instead they used levers to insert a timber platform, or raft, underneath each stone, then gradually built up the platform from underneath. These monuments were almost certainly designed for religious ceremonies honouring the sun or the moon, but we do not know precisely how they were used.

LAKE VILLAGES

In some parts of Europe, especially Switzerland and northern Italy, people built artificial islands in the middle of deep lakes. They were the safest sites for new village homes. Villagers travelled to and from their fields by boat or walked across well-defended bridges of stones and pounded earth, which linked the villages with the shore.

▲ Stonehenge, a huge circle-shaped monument in southern England. It was rebuilt and enlarged between about 2100 and 1500 BC. The outer ring measures almost 30 metres across. There are 30 standing stones, called sarsens, all about 4 metres high.

ARCTIC INVENTIONS

Because most American people left no written records, it is hard to know exactly when they made many of their inventions and discoveries. But archaeologists use scientific techniques, such as radio-carbon dating, to help them find out. Their results suggest that by about 1600 BC Native peoples in Arctic North America had invented long-bladed knives made of bone, walrus ivory and wood to cut large blocks of snow for building some of the first ever igloos. Archaeologists have also found the remains of well-designed kayaks. These are sea-going canoes, used to hunt seals and walrus, and were first used about 1500 BC.

JADE AND PYRAMIDS

In Central America in about 1200 BC, the Olmec people of Mexico became very skilled at carving jade – an extremely hard stone. First the jade block was roughly cut using a mallet made from stone. Then the shape was hollowed out and finely polished with grains of wet sand. They used the sand to rub away at the surface, because they did not have metal tools. This was very slow and took a lot of hard work. Enormous amounts of labour were also needed to build the Olmecs' pyramid-shaped temples. Archaeologists have worked out that it took 800,000 working days to build the largest pyramid, which dates from around 900 BC.

Olmec scholars were very skilful astronomers. They worked out a calendar based on the movements of the sun and the moon and invented a system of picture-writing to record what they had seen.

◀ This mask of jade was made by Olmec craftworkers, probably for a priest or a king to wear. Fine, very delicate objects like this took many months to make.

PET DINGOES

AUSTRALASIA

Wolf-like dogs called dingoes were first brought to Australia around 2000 BC, probably by traders from South Asia. Dingoes could be trained as guard dogs, but were mostly treated as pets, especially by women whose babies had died. They were also used to provide warmth in bed like modern hot-water bottles. A traditional Aboriginal saying describes a chilly winter night as 'five-dog weather'.

▲ This picture of an Aboriginal campsite was painted in the nineteenth century. You can see two dingoes sitting by the campfire.

DEATH SPEARS

Around the same time, Aboriginal warriors invented new weapons, and used them in battles to conquer new land. Death spears were sticks covered with tiny, razor-sharp blades. They were designed to make their victim bleed to death. A spear-thrower, called a woomera, was used to throw spears over a long distance.

THE CREATIVE WORLD

▲ This gold ornament is shaped like an eagle with outstretched wings. It was found in the tomb of a Phoenician king. He would have worn it across his chest.

Sometimes people looking back into the past think that societies long ago were primitive and unskilled. This is not true. The people of Tutankhamun's time had not invented many of the machines that make life easy in the modern world. They had no motors and no electricity, no televisions or computers or cars. But they survived without all the technology that helps us today. They not only survived, but using the simplest of tools they created huge buildings that have lasted thousands of years, and beautiful works of art that people still admire.

◀ A tomb painting from Egypt. It shows a dead man and his wife in the next world. They are listening to a musician who is playing the harp and singing. Rich Egyptian people enjoyed watching all kinds of entertainers at parties and feasts, including singers, dancers, jugglers and acrobats.

PALACES AND TOMBS

AFRICA

The treasures found in Tutankhamun's tomb show the skills of Egyptian artists. These people made beautiful jewels, weapons, furniture, vases, statues and wall-paintings to enrich the pharaohs' palaces, temples and tombs. They used gold, bronze, turquoise and cedar wood, brought to their workshops from hundreds of kilometres away. Hard building stone was often found nearby, but it took thousands of hours of patient work with simple copper, wood and stone tools to produce temple figures of pharaohs and gods, or delicate carvings to decorate palace walls.

BRONZE AND JADE

EAST ASIA

In China, craftworkers made bronze vessels in all kinds of shapes to hold religious offerings. Some looked like animals, others like monsters. Chinese craftworkers also carved objects out of the precious green stone called jade, and they made pottery jugs and dishes in fantastic shapes, with delicate decorations. At first these were made for everyday use by kings and nobles, but the best examples were later collected as works of art, just to be admired.

ROYAL TREASURES

MIDDLE EAST

The arts and crafts of many Middle Eastern lands show the luxurious lifestyle of rich and powerful kings. Many everyday items used by royal families in their palaces have survived, as well as crowns, weapons and jewellery, such as the eagle ornament opposite. Even drinking cups and musical instruments were often beautifully decorated, or trimmed with gold.

Middle Eastern kings also commissioned splendid buildings including ziggurats (pyramid-shaped temples) and palaces with gardens and lakes. Scribes found time to write down religious texts and ancient legends – like the story of Gilgamesh, a mighty hero, who had all kinds of adventures in the kingdom of the gods.

▲ There is a lot of fine detail in this work. It is made from red-coloured gold and shows an Egyptian pharaoh riding in his chariot.

◄ A Chinese wine container, made from bronze and shaped like an owl. It was made around 1100 BC.

▶ A stone seal carved with an elephant, made at Mohenjo-Daro in the Indus Valley. The most beautiful seals were worn on necklaces or around the wrist.

FINE DECORATION

In northern Europe stone monuments such as Stonehenge (see page 34) were built or rebuilt in Tutankhamun's time. They still impress us today with their size and with the boldness and strength of their design. But European craftworkers were also capable of detailed, delicate work. They made necklaces out of smooth, shiny amber, which they collected from the seashore, and collars and bracelets of glittering gold. They cast finely decorated swords, axes, helmets and shields by pouring molten bronze into carved stone moulds.

◀ Artists took many of their ideas from the world around them. This pottery jar from Mycenae, Greece, is painted with an octopus design.

ALL KINDS OF CRAFTS

Visitors to the workshops at Mohenjo-Daro, the biggest city in the Indus Valley region, would have met many different craftsmen and women: metalworkers, potters, bead-makers and clothmakers. Stonecarvers engraved scenes of religious worship or everyday life on to tiny seal stones, about 2.5 centimetres long. When these seal stones were pressed into melted wax, they left a little picture. Seals were used to approve documents or to seal bags holding valuable goods. Craftworkers also made toys, whistles and lifelike statues out of clay. All these goods were traded with other Indus Valley cities and with neighbouring lands. Examples of standardized weights and measures, to stop traders cheating, have also been found in Indus Valley sites.

PAINTINGS AND POTTERY

In southern Europe many wall-paintings, statues and painted pots have survived to tell us about the people who lived in the rich Minoan and Mycenean civilizations of Greece, and what kinds of decorations they admired. Artists painted frescoes using paint and water on damp plaster walls to create very fresh colours. There is an example on page 15. On mainland Greece, kings and chieftains lived in well-defended palaces, decorated with carved lions and other ferocious creatures, which were designed to show off a ruler's strength and power. Kings were buried with a large quantity of rich grave goods so they could go on enjoying their treasures in the kingdom of the dead.

EARTHWORKS AND WEAVING

In several parts of America massive earthworks and huge stone monuments were an important form of art. They still survive today at Chavin de Huantar in Peru and in south-eastern North America. Some of the earliest South American pottery and cloth was made in Peru between 2000 and 1000 BC. Weavers in Peru were usually women. They made beautiful fabrics, often patterned with designs of jaguars, and woven in strong colours that can still be seen today.

MAGIC SCENES

The Aboriginal peoples of Australia carved and painted scenes from the Dreamtime on rocks and in caves, showing ancestor-spirits, animals and people hunting or dancing. Some artists painted in a lifelike way. Others painted people with their bones visible through their skins, like modern X-rays. These paintings are some of the oldest pictures in the world. The earliest were made almost 40,000 years before the time of Tutankhamun, although they were still being created during his reign.

Artists used two methods to create pictures. They either rubbed coloured earth on to the cave's rocky walls, or they crushed the earth to a fine powder and blew it through pipes to make patterns on the surface of the cave wall.

▲ An Aboriginal painting from Nourlangie Rock, Australia. It shows figures from the Dreamtime, painted in X-ray style.

► This painted pot shows women weaving cloth on a backstrap loom – a simple, lightweight, portable invention that is still used today.

BELIEFS AND IDEAS

▲ This necklace from Tutankhamun's tomb is decorated with gold and stone scarab beetles. These beetles collect little balls of dung and roll them across the ground. The Egyptians thought they were holy creatures because their movements were like the movements of the sun-god as he rolled the sun across the sky.

People living in the time of Tutankhamun thought the world was a frightening and unpredictable place. When floods, earthquakes and storms wrecked fields and farms and disease killed thousands of people, no one understood why. They felt helpless, and feared they had upset the gods or the invisible spirits who controlled their land. To stop these disasters happening again, they held ceremonies to please the gods and spirits, and offered them gifts of their most precious things: their children, their best animals, wine and food.

People living in different parts of the world worshipped their own special gods and goddesses in lots of different ways. But they usually shared many of the same beliefs and fears. Often, they tried to get close to their gods by singing, dancing, meditating or taking drugs. To prepare for these religious ceremonies they purified themselves by taking special baths or fasting.

◄ An Egyptian painting on papyrus shows the dog-headed god, Anubis, making a mummy. The storage jars beneath the mummy hold the dead person's heart, liver and other organs.

LIFE AND DEATH

The Egyptians believed in life after death. That is why they preserved peoples' bodies as mummies. They thought that a person's spirit would live in the next world only for as long as his or her mummified body survived. First the body was washed and the organs removed. Then it was dried out, using a chemical called natron, and refilled with sawdust, linen, resin and natron. Finally, the body was wrapped in linen. Mummies of pharaohs had to be done very well so they would live for ever. Ordinary people were not mummified, but buried in the desert.

POWERFUL GODS

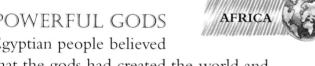

AFRICA

Egyptian people believed that the gods had created the world and continued to rule it, so everyone had to live by their laws. This meant fighting bravely, working hard and making offerings to the gods. The Ancient Egyptians worshipped many different gods and goddesses. Each one looked after a particular part of daily life, or was linked to powerful natural forces, such as the sun or storms.

SACRED SPIRITS

Many African people were animists. This meant that they believed all living and natural things, including rocks and mountains, had powerful spirits. They made offerings to please these spirits, or ask for their help. They also honoured their dead ancestors, who had the power to bring disaster if angered or ignored. African priests performed ceremonies to see into the future and to drive away evil spirits.

► Egyptian craftworkers made wooden boxes to hold shabti figures. These were buried with mummies to look after them in the kingdom of the dead. The box is decorated with a picture of a priestess kneeling in front of Nut, the goddess of the sycamore tree.

STAIRWAYS TO HEAVEN

MIDDLE EAST

The peoples of Mesopotamia worshipped gods and goddesses with many different powers. Marduk made crops grow, Sin was god of the moon, and Ishtar was goddess of war. The gods protected individual men and women, and whole cities too. But they also had terrible powers to punish or destroy. Mesopotamian people offered sacrifices and said prayers at the top of huge ziggurats. These were pyramid-shaped temples, built as high as possible to reach up to the gods. People called them 'stairways to heaven'.

► A carved stone stele (pillar), made around 1900 BC in Canaan. It shows the god Baal, lord of storms. He is armed with a thunderbolt, ready to attack his enemies.

▲ The Great Ziggurat at Ur, in present-day Iran, was built around 2100 BC. It was still used for ceremonies hundreds of years later, in Tutankhamun's day.

HIGH ALTARS

In Canaan and nearby lands the Philistines worshipped El, god of the sky, Baal, god of winds and thunder, and Baal's wife, Astarte, goddess of love. To feel nearer to the gods, the Philistines built altars on top of high hills. The Jews, who lived in Israel, were unlike many other Middle Eastern peoples. They worshipped only one god. They called him Yaweh.

ORACLE BONES

EAST ASIA

In Shang times, Chinese people believed in a supreme god called Shang Di, who lived in the sky. He sent blessings to people on earth, especially to the Shang emperor, whose official name was 'son of heaven'. The emperors had to act as a link between heaven and earth by saying prayers and offering sacrifices.

Each Chinese family also believed that the spirits of dead ancestors had the power to help or harm them. The Shang emperors often asked their ancestors for advice. They wrote messages on animal bones or tortoise shells, then heated them. They believed the pattern of cracks that appeared would tell them the future.

◄ An oracle bone from the Shang Dynasty in China. You can see the cracks made when it was heated, over 3,000 years ago.

THE ARYANS

In about 1500 BC, invaders known as the Aryan people brought a new religion to northern India. They worshipped nature gods such as Indra, god of the sky, Agni, god of fire, Surya the sun god, and Yama, god of death. Aryan priests and poets composed a series of religious songs known as the Rig Veda, which means Verses of Knowledge. They are among the oldest surviving poems in the world, and tell stories about gods and heroes. Because ordinary people could not read or write, poems and songs were the best way of teaching everyone about beliefs and ideas.

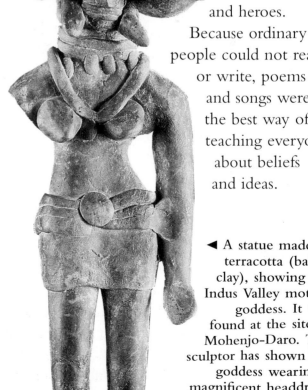

SUN WORSHIPPERS

In Japan, the ancient national religion was called Shinto. It was based on the worship of gods and nature spirits, such as Amaterasu, the sun goddess. Shinto taught that every natural object had a spirit, and that these should be respected. Japanese people also honoured their emperors, and believed they were descended from the sun goddess. Family ancestors and national heroes were also honoured as if they were almost gods.

MOTHER OF THE WORLD

SOUTH ASIA

The Indus Valley people worshipped a goddess they called Mother of the World. She gave life to all creatures. They also worshipped a male god. We don't know his name, but he later became known as Shiva in the Hindu faith. He was worshipped as both a creator and a destroyer. One of his names was Lord of the Dance.

Fire and water were important in Indus Valley religious ceremonies. People killed animals and burned them as offerings. Priests and priest-kings purified themselves in sacred baths before taking part in religious rituals. Further south, Indian worshippers honoured idols by sprinkling them with perfume and decorating them with flowers.

◄ A statue made of terracotta (baked clay), showing the Indus Valley mother goddess. It was found at the site of Mohenjo-Daro. The sculptor has shown the goddess wearing a magnificent headdress, several necklaces, and a short skirt.

CELTIC GODS

In northern Europe some early Celtic peoples believed in many different gods and goddesses, who protected and helped them. In return, the Celts offered sacrifices to the gods of horses, weapons, jewels and people. Victims for sacrifice were thrown into lakes or bogs. The Celts also preserved the skulls of ancestors and enemies. They believed that a person's spirit stayed in the head after death, and would protect the living.

BULL-LEAPING

In Crete, palaces were built with central courtyards where bull-leaping ceremonies were held. Specially-trained athletes captured from conquered cities had to vault through the horns of a bull as it charged around. This was terribly dangerous, and many athletes died. At the end of the ceremony the bull was also killed. The Cretans believed that this bloodshed helped to bring a good harvest the following year.

JAGUAR BABY

The many different peoples of North America all had similar religious ideas. They respected the living world and tried to live in harmony with it. They honoured Mother Earth and the invisible spirits in mountains, winds and trees. Totem animals were important, too. They guided and protected individuals and tribes.

In Central America, the Olmecs carved many images of their special god – a were-jaguar. He was half human baby, half wild cat. He was powerful and bloodthirsty, with fearsome fangs. The Olmecs also worshipped other fierce animal gods. These were based on the animals that lived in the rainforest around them, including alligators, snakes and sharks.

▼ This fresco (wall-painting) was made for the palace of King Minos in Crete. It shows three athletes taking part in the bull-leaping ritual to bring a good harvest.

▲ In this Olmec stone carving you can see a king carrying a were-jaguar god in his arms. Carvings like this show that the Olmecs believed some of their kings were descended from the gods and had magical powers, including being able to turn into were-jaguars.

GODS FOR SURVIVAL

In South America, people said prayers to a creator god. They believed he was ruler of the world and lord of the sun. In the Andes region, they called him Viracocha, but people gave him different names elsewhere.

South American people also honoured many other nature-gods, who sent good harvests and life-giving rain. These were essential for survival, so South American priests and people took part in special ceremonies at important times in the farming year, such as planting seeds, or harvest. They also offered sacrifices of people or blood to feed the gods.

DREAMTIME

In Australia, religious beliefs came from the idea of the Dreamtime. This was a magical era when the Ancestors of all living creatures walked and danced on earth. The Ancestors bound together all parts of creation – land, sky, water, people, animals and plants – to make a peaceful whole. Aboriginal people held religious ceremonies at holy sites, such as the great rock Uluru, recreating their Ancestors' dances to maintain good order in the living world.

NATURE GODS

In the islands of the Pacific Ocean, people were afraid of the powerful creatures around them, such as sharks, and of natural forces, such as lightning and volcanoes. They thought of these as nature-gods, and made images to honour them so that the natural world would not harm them.

► A modern carving of a sea-spirit with a shark's head. It is made from wood and comes from the Solomon Islands in the Pacific Ocean. There are no ancient carvings like these left, because wood does not last as long as stone, but the traditions continue.

PEOPLES FROM AROUND THE WORLD

Aboriginals The first inhabitants of Australia, who arrived there about 40,000 years ago.

Aryans A sub-group of the Indo-European people. They migrated to India around 1500 BC.

Bantu People who lived in the rainforests and plains of central and southern Africa.

Celts Hunters and farmers who lived in northern Europe.

Chavin Farmers who lived in the mountains of Peru around 1500 BC.

Hittites People who settled in Anatolia (present-day Turkey) around 2000 BC.

Hyksos Groups of invaders from Asia who ruled Egypt about 150 years before Tutankhamun was born.

Indo-Europeans A term to describe many prehistoric peoples of Europe, Central Asia and North India.

Inuit Native Americans who arrived in the Arctic regions of North America from Siberia around 2000 BC.

Jews People who settled in Judah (parts of present-day Palestine, Israel, Syria and Jordan) around 1000 BC.

Khoisan Nomad hunters and gatherers from southern Africa.

Minoans The people who lived on the Mediterranean island of Crete from around 2000–1450 BC.

Myceneans People who lived in and around the city-state of Mycenae, southern Greece, from about 1600–1100 BC.

Mongols Nomads from the grassy plains north of China.

Native Americans The first inhabitants of America, who arrived there about 30,000 years ago. Native American people were divided into many nations, with different lifestyles and languages.

Olmecs The people who lived in the rainforests of southern Mexico from around 2000 BC.

Pacific peoples People who lived on islands in the Pacific Ocean. They were descended from settlers who migrated there from South and East Asia.

Phoenicians People who lived along the eastern Mediterranean coast. From around 1100 BC they built up a rich trading empire.

Sumerians People who settled in southern Mesopotamia from around 3000 BC. They built some of the world's earliest cities and invented writing.

alpaca South American animal of the camel family.

amber Sticky, yellowish gum produced by trees. Over many years it becomes hard and is used to make jewellery.

archaeologist A person who studies the ancient past by digging up remains.

astronomer A scientist who studies the stars and planets.

burial mound A mound, usually made of earth, under which people were buried.

calculation Mathematical workings out.

cast To shape liquid metal or glass by pouring it into a mould.

ceremony A formal gathering of people, often with music, held in honour of a special event.

chariot A two-wheeled vehicle pulled by horses.

chieftain Leader of a tribe or group of people often related by birth or marriage.

city-state A city or town, together with the surrounding farms and fields.

civilization A society with its own laws, customs, beliefs and artistic traditions.

cocoon A small pouch of silky thread made by insects in which their grubs develop.

code A series of laws or rules gathered into one set of instructions.

democratic Describes a country in which the people choose the leaders who govern them.

dye A mixture used to colour things. In Tutankhamun's time, dyes were made of plants, crushed rocks and metal shavings.

earthwork A large mound, ditch, bank or circle that is made of earth dug from the land around.
embroidered Decorated with patterns and pictures sewn in coloured threads.
empire A large area of land, including several different nations or peoples, governed by a single ruler called an emperor.
engrave Cut into a hard surface.

fortress A building that is strongly defended against attack.

gourds Plants with fruits that can be dried, hollowed out, and used as containers.
grave goods Valuable objects buried alongside a dead person.

hemp Rough cloth made from plant fibres.
hieroglyphs Ancient Egyptian picture writing.
Hindu A follower of the Hindu religion, which began in India between around 1500 and 600 BC. Hindus worship many gods, but they are all forms of Brahman, the supreme god.

inlaid Set into a surface.
irrigation The channelling of water into dry land so that crops can grow there.
ivory The hard substance that elephant and walrus tusks are made of.

llama South American animal of the camel family.

meditate Think deeply about spiritual things.
memorial A building or object made in honour of a dead person or past event.
Middle East The term used to describe an area stretching east from the Mediterranean Sea.
migration The movement of many people together in search of new lands.
mummy A body that has been specially preserved before burial.

navigate To plot a course at sea and steer a ship along it.
nomads People who have no settled home, and who move from place to place in search of food or grazing land.

oracle A telling of future events through special signs.

papyrus Paper made from the papyrus reed.
pharaoh The name for a king in Ancient Egypt.
plantain A kind of banana-like fruit with a green skin.
primitive Lacking knowledge or skills.
pulley A wheel with a grooved rim in which a rope can run. A series of pulleys can be used to lift heavy loads.
purify To free oneself from bad behaviour or thoughts. People thought they could do this by washing or going without food.

radio-carbon dating A way of discovering how old some remains are by measuring the amount of radioactive carbon in them.
resin Sticky gum produced by trees.

ritual Traditional way of marking a special, often religious, event.

sacrifice An offering made to please the gods.
scholar Someone who spends their life studying.
scribe A specially-trained person who kept written records of events, business deals, laws and so on.
scroll Word used for a roll of paper, parchment or papyrus.
seal Stamp or design pressed into clay or wax to show ownership or official approval.
sesame A plant grown for its seeds, which are eaten or crushed to make oil.
shaman A magic healer.
sickle A curved knife used to cut crops.
squash A food plant similar to a pumpkin.
sundial A kind of clock that uses the sun's shadow to tell the time.
survey To measure land by working out distances and area mathematically.

technology The science of developing tools and techniques to meet practical needs.
teepee The Native American name for a tent made of animal skins and wooden poles.
totem An object that represents a family or tribe.
tribe A group of peoples of the same race and culture.

vizier An important official in the Egyptian government.

warlord A warrior leader who controls parts of a country.

yam A kind of root vegetable.

INDEX